Hans Joachim Barschel
A Design Pioneer
in Our Midst

R. ROGER REMINGTON

HANS J.

BARSCHEL

Hans Joachim Barschel

A Design Pioneer
in Our Midst

R. ROGER REMINGTON

GRAPHIC DESIGN ARCHIVES

CHAPBOOK SERIES: EIGHT

RIT PRESS

2025

Hans Joachim Barschel
A Design Pioneer in Our Midst

BY R. ROGER REMINGTON

GRAPHIC DESIGN ARCHIVES
CHAPBOOK SERIES: EIGHT

We gather on the traditional territory of the Onöndowa'ga:' or "the people of the Great Hill." In English, they are known as Seneca people, "the keeper of the western door." They are one of the six nations that make up the sovereign Haudenosaunee Confederacy.

We honor the land on which RIT was built and recognize the unique relationship that the Indigenous stewards have with this land. That relationship is the core of their traditions, cultures, and histories. We recognize the history of genocide, colonization, and assimilation of Indigenous people that took place on this land. Mindful of these histories, we work towards understanding, acknowledging, and ultimately reconciliation.

Cover: Joe Neil, "Prof. Hans J. Barschel schaut uber eines seiner mit Kasein gemalten s.g. MICRO ABSTRACT Entwrfen" (Prof. Hans J. Barschel looks over one of his so-called MICRO ABSTRACT designs painted with casein), 1974, 6 × 4.75 in.

Published and distributed by:
RIT Press
90 Lomb Memorial Drive
Rochester, New York 14623
https://press.rit.edu

ISBN 978-1-956313-09-3 (print)
ISBN 978-1-956313-10-9 (electronic)
Printed in the USA

Library of Congress Cataloging-in-Publication Data

Names:	Remington, R. Roger, author.
Title:	Hans Joachim Barschel : a design pioneer in our midst / R. Roger Remington.
Description:	Rochester, New York : RIT Press, [2025]	Series: Graphic design archives chapbook series	Includes bibliographical references.
Identifiers:	LCCN 2023048264	ISBN 9781956313093 (paperback)	ISBN 9781956313109 (ebook)
Subjects: LCSH:	Barschel, Hans Joachim, 1912–	Graphic artists—United States—Biography.	Rochester Institute of Technology—Faculty—Biography.
Classification:	LCC NC999.4.B37 R46 2024	DDC 744.092—dc23/eng/20231120

LC record available at https://lccn.loc.gov/2023048264

Hans Joachim Barschel
A Design Pioneer in Our Midst

R. ROGER REMINGTON

VIGNELLI DISTINGUISHED PROFESSOR OF DESIGN EMERITUS

ROCHESTER INSTITUTE OF TECHNOLOGY

His Personal Journey: From Berlin to New York to Rochester
Both native-born and immigrant men and women shaped
the history of graphic design in America, particularly in the
Modernist era. One individual who deserves more attention is
German designer Hans Joachim Barschel (1912–1998).
His singular design accomplishments furthered the Modernist
impact on American graphic design. Earlier, in Berlin, he had
begun a flourishing professional career, which expanded
on his arrival in New York in 1938. Eventually, new design
opportunities arose that led him to practice design in a different
setting, then move on to share his extensive experience with
students as a professor at Rochester Institute of Technology.

His story is the important narrative of a talented and creative
visual designer, who, like others, found his way to a promising
environment in which to begin new career challenges.
For fifteen years in New York City, he devoted himself to a
significant professional graphic-design practice in a strongly
competitive business environment. In time, he chose to pass
on knowledge and skills to others as a teacher. What follows
is a documentation of preparation, practice, risk-taking,
dedication, exploration, and professional accomplishment
by this designer, who, through his design and teaching,
contributed significantly to the design field and touched the
lives of many around him.

Left

Immigrants arriving at Ellis Island in New York, c. 1907, Archive Pics / Alamy Stock Photo. A wave of architects, art directors, and designers immigrated to the United States of America as the nation emerged from the Great Depression across the 1920s and 1930s, including Hans Joachim Barschel in 1937.

"Nearly all Americans have ancestors who braved the oceans–liberty-loving risk takers in search of an ideal–the largest voluntary migrations in recorded history... Immigration is not just a link to America's past; it's also a bridge to America's future."

President George Bush

1 Lauren Schwaar, "Difficulties Faced by Immigrants and Refugees," *Life and Light Magazine*, 2015.

2 Otto Friedrich, *Before the Deluge*, 1972, 391.

Immigrants to America: New Beginnings from the Old

In his biography of the legendary magazine art director Alexey Brodovitch, writer Andy Grundberg referred to a select group of European creatives as having an "Émigré Mind." Many Europeans shared a common notion of emigrating to America. For them, America was promise. The reality was that the immigrant needed financial resources to begin to consider this quest. In America, many fresh arrivals faced serious challenges they had never anticipated, such as legal complications, transportation issues, lodging challenges, psychological distress, and depression. Those new to America had to form new habits and leave former behaviors behind.

The shock of change was often unsettling. It took great courage to abandon familiar practices of everyday life. "The process of crossing cultures challenges the very basis of who we are as cultural beings."[1] Challenges were never-ending for the immigrant. Upon arrival in a totally new environment, each individual had to trust that life would be better and that there would be opportunity ahead. For many new immigrants, "the desire to live one's own life as best as one can, to do one's own work and raise one's own children, is not a contemptible emotion."[2] The American environment was alluring and full of possibility to many designers. Commercial art and illustration for advertising were the dominant features of the American graphics scene. Many Europeans looked to America as a "blank slate," upon which they could make their mark and immediately apply their Modernist approaches to the needs of business and industry.

In the United States, the quality of design was greatly enhanced by the arrival of designers from Europe who had been steeped in the dynamic influence of avant-garde thinking. These creators, in assessing the reality of American graphic design, saw great opportunity for innovation. Immigrant architect Paul T. Frankl described his initial feelings and provided a glimpse of what lay ahead.

> My visits to the States had been all I could have wished for and a great deal more. My eyes had beheld the beauty that was America. I saw much and learned even more, but my search for new expressions in architecture was in vain. Instead I discovered the greatest country in the world, unaware of its greatness, copying the meaningless outworn forms of architecture and design of bygone days and bygone countries, a giant, slumbering, waiting to be awakened to lead the world.[3]

Designers in Europe looked to America as a place of great promise. Erich Mendelsohn's 1928 publication *Amerika: Bilderbuch eines Architekten*, the first book about the International Style in American architecture, showed, through photographs, America's potential. The great Russian Constructivist designer El Lissitzky was so impressed with Mendelsohn's book that he said the volume "thrills us like a dramatic film. Before our eyes move pictures that are absolutely unique."[4] America was very appealing to many Europeans.

3 Alison Sharp and Elana Shapira, *Émigré Cultures*, 2017, 34.

4 Erich Mendelsohn, *Amerika: Bilderbuch eines Architekten*, 1924.

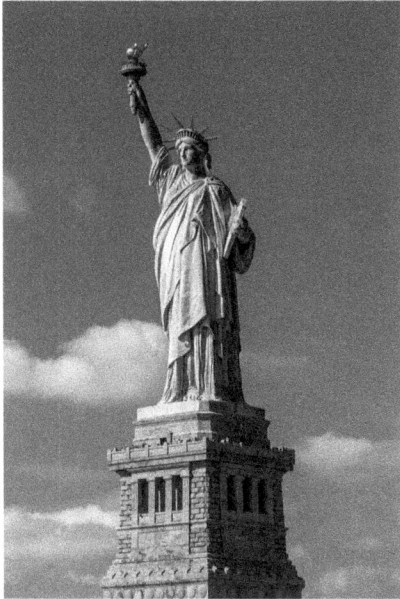

Statue of Liberty, New York City.
Nido Huebl / Adobe Stock.

Among the earliest in this wave of immigrant designers was Cipe Pineles, who arrived from Austria in 1921 and would go on to be the only female magazine art director of her time. Other early arrivals were architects Richard Neutra and Knut Lonberg-Holm. Dr. Mehemed Fehmy Agha came from Berlin in 1929 at the invitation of Mr. Condé Nast to become the art director of *Vogue* magazine. The *Condé Nast* magazine empire at that time also included *Vanity Fair* and *House and Garden* magazine. In 1930, John Story Jenks hired Alexey Brodovitch away from his work in Paris to come to Philadelphia and teach at the Pennsylvania Museum School of Industrial Art. Eventually, Brodovitch was lured to New York to become the art director at *Harper's Bazaar* magazine. As the decade wore on, with the tumultuous geopolitical challenges in Europe, many other important designers found their way to the United States to begin their careers anew. Included in this later group were architects Walter Gropius, Marcel Breuer, Mies van der Rohe, and Frederick Keisler. Other artists and designers were Joseph Albers, Eva Zeisel, Walter Allner, George Grosz, Laszlo Moholy-Nagy, Gyorgy Kepes, Joseph Binder, Herbert Bayer, Richard Huelsenbeck, Will Burtin, George Giusti, Alexander Liberman, George Tscherny, George and Stephan Salter, Leo Lionni, Herbert Matter, Domenico Poulon, Peter Piening, Xanti Schawinsky, and Ladislav Sutnar. Also among this group of immigrant designers was Hans Barschel. He and his colleagues encountered people and opportunities that permitted them to become a force for transforming design in America–supporting business, industry, and education as the nation emerged from the Great Depression.

5   Erik Larson, *In the Garden of Beasts*, 2011, 56.

6   Smithsonian Archives of American Art, Oral History interview with Hans Barschel, 1994.

Barschel: Beginnings in Berlin

Hans Barschel spent the first twenty-five years of his life in Berlin, Germany. Born in 1912 in exclusive Charlottenburg and growing up in the Pankow neighborhoods of suburban Berlin, he rebelled early in his life against the oppressive remnants of the Victorian era around him, especially many of his traditional family values. His father was a civil engineer, but Barschel felt his destiny was to "look for a new sort of life." He recalled, "I was born at the end of the German Victorian era."[5] He was not very fond of school, except for classes in drawing, modern languages, and the natural sciences. His Aunt Else was a free spirit and promoted young Barschel's self-expression.

Berlin in those days was active with avant-garde creativity, especially in the arts. Eventually, typical of many young and progressive students of the time, he found, as an undergraduate at the Berlin Municipal Art School (Kunstgewerbeschule), a direction toward a Modernist view. There he studied with eminent book designer George Salter. An enlightened instructor, Salter presented a loose curriculum to which his student Barschel strongly related. Barschel thought the world of his teacher Salter.

> He was the greatest book-jacket designer of any in Berlin. A very sensitive artist, the way he designed his book-jackets was exceptional. He was a great inspiration for me, in what he could do and with whom he could work. I got from him my first book-jacket assignments from publishers in Berlin. Later I helped him to get away from the Nazis. He was Jewish, and he had already fled to Baden-Baden, and the Nazis were after him. I informed him secretly, and he fled from Baden-Baden to America.[6]

HANS-JOACHIMS

WERDEGANG

1912.   1927.

mit Jllustrationen

von

TANTE ELSE.

Druck und Verlag Loebrie, Tempelhof.

- 7 -

Die Spielsachen hielt in Ordnung er all,
Am schönsten war Grosspapas Pferdestall,
Ein Kunstwerk, prächtig anzuschauen,
Noch heut kann ein jeder sich dran erbauen!-

So hat es ihm also an nichts gefehlt,
Nur Tante Else hat oft ihn gequält,
Von klein auf wollt' sie ihn schon dressieren
Zum Stillstehen beim Photographieren.
War dies zuweilen ihm auch ein Graus,
Hielt er doch geduldig und tapfer aus.
Damit man sieht, wie gut er trainiert,
Hab' seinen Werdegang hier illustriert.-

Berlin, Tauentzienstraße with car traffic, 1926. Photo: Willem van de Poll, National Archives / Van de Poll collection.

"If New York is a wise guy,
Paris a coquette, Rome a gigolo
and Berlin a wicked uncle,
then London is an old lady who
mutters and has the second sight.
She is slightly deaf, and doesn't
suffer fools gladly."

Adrian Anthony Gill

Hans Barschel's parents, 1938,
24 × 17.5 cm.

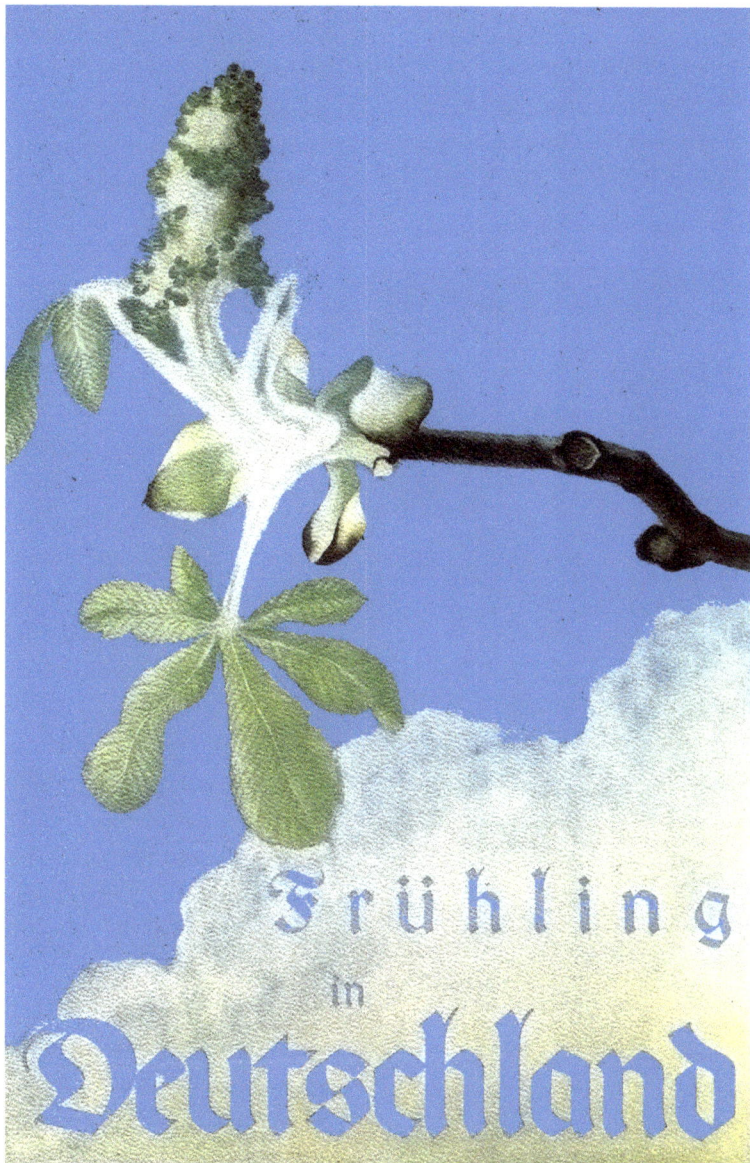

Top to bottom and right
Hans Barschel at seven years old, 1919,
23.5 × 17.5 cm.

Tanta (Aunt) Else, taken from *Hans-Joachims Werdegang* (career), c. 1927,
scrapbook, 4 × 4 cm.

Frühling in Deutschland (poster
announcing spring in Germany),
from *PM* volume 4, number 6, 1938,
14 × 19 cm.

7 R. Roger Remington, personal video interview with Hans Barschel, 1984.

8 R. Roger Remington, personal interview with Hans Barschel, 1985.

"Zuverlassig! Deutsche Reichsbahn" (Reliable! German Railways), 1935, poster, 81.2 × 58.4 cm.

A decade later, Salter was to mentor Barschel on the other side of the Atlantic in New York. Subsequent to his studies at the Berlin Municipal Art School, Barschel studied at the State Academy of Fine and Applied Arts (Kunsthochschule) in Berlin-Charlottenberg. Here he completed postgraduate studies with Professor Ernst Boehm, who was "more nature-oriented, also an artist/designer good in pattern designs and fabrics."[7] Barschel studied design, painting, printmaking, and photography. Thus were sown the early seeds of Barschel's multimedia approach to creative expression.

Traveling Europe in the 1930s was by rail. For many, it had a glamour and mystique that continues to this day. The dynamic qualities of speed, color, intensity; the metal-clanging, steam-hissing, smoke-belching, massive iron-moving machines—coupled with a comfortably quiet, fast ride—made for an appealing travel experience. In film as well as in books and posters, the train was romanticized and popularized. Barschel was among those designers, worldwide, who shared in the allure of the railroad and saw trains as a powerful subject for visual interpretation. While he was in graduate school, his renderings of trains and railroads were a major part of his studies and eventually became his thesis project. From a faculty committee involved in reviewing his finished work, Barschel learned that the promotional director of Reichsbahn Advertising Office (Deutsche Reichsbahn Werbeamt) was on site at the school. After the project critique, the director, impressed with Barschel's graphics, "took me in his Mercedes to his office to give me my first graphics assignment, a poster showing the dynamic driving wheels of a glamorous steam engine."[8] This happened in 1935 and was a dramatic professional launch.

9 Steven Heller, "O.H.W. Hadank,
   The Classicist Even a Modernist
   Could Love," unpublished essay.

Below, left to right
Personal branding project for Professor
Hadank: a graphic translation of "Barch"
fish to stand for Barschel, c. 1934,
4 × 3.5 cm.

Application of "Barch" mark to personal
stationery, c. 1934, 20.7 × 10.3 cm.

A new mentor entered Barschel's life soon after. Barschel was
fortunate in having classes with Professor O.H.W. Hadank,
one of the most prominent and progressive Berlin graphic
designers of the time. A freelance designer, Hadank produced
packaging design, labels, and, in particular, trademarks.
He developed a distinctive Modernist style of his own, using
symbolic forms in his graphic-design solutions for clients.
Barschel recalled, "He was famous for his Ravenklau
cigarette packages, which were fantastic, really, exquisite."[9]
Paul Rand, a major figure in Modernist graphic design in
America, considered Hadank an important pioneer and later
credited him as one of his own important influences. Design-
history writer Steven Heller wrote about Hadank as a teacher:
"The lesson Hadank taught his students was this: style for
style's sake is irrelevant. Type and image must function well
in its printed environment."

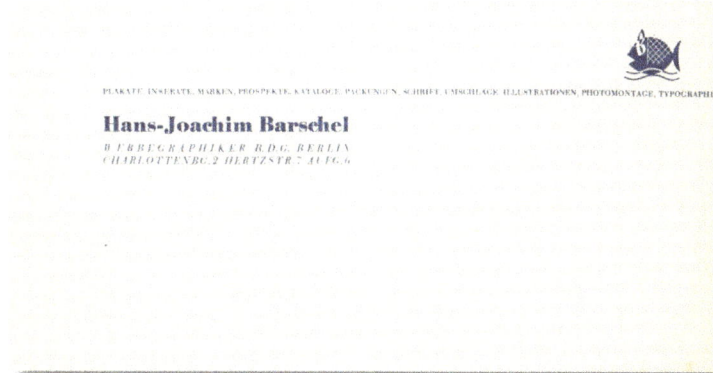

PLAKATE, INSERATE, MARKEN, PROSPEKTE, KATALOGE, PACKUNGEN, SCHRIFT, UMSCHLAGE, ILLUSTRATIONEN, PHOTOMONTAGE, TYPOGRAPHIE

Hans-Joachim Barschel
GEBRAUCHSGRAPHIKER B.D.G. BERLIN
CHARLOTTENBG.2 HERTZSTR.7 AUFG.6

10 R. Roger Remington, personal
    interview with Hans Barschel, 1985.

Barschel recalled a graduate class project that involved designing a personal logotype: "I based my design on a plump and bony fish common in the waters around Berlin called a Barch. This poor fish is so bony that Berliners use it to make a succulent fish soup and then give the rest to the cat." Through Professor Hadank, Barschel was exposed to the necessary disciplines of being a professional designer.

Fresh out of school, Barschel and several talented classmates were selected by the Berlin public transportation system to design three large murals in a key subway station. Their selection was the result of a competition among young designers. Hitler was dressing up Berlin for the 1936 Olympiad, and there would be much public exposure to the proposed murals.

Hans Barschel painting murals for a Berlin subway station, 1936, 13.6 × 8.5 cm.

As a recent graduate, Barschel was afforded great visibility as well as a presence in the Berlin graphic-design community. Soon, yet another challenge would present itself to the young designer. A Jewish colleague, who was working for an architecture office, asked Barschel to make a delivery for him. The Nazis sent a car, with all the swastika flags flying, for Barschel. On arriving at the office of the client and with the Nazi salute and clicking heels, Barschel realized that he was soon to face the Führer. Hitler expressed disdain with the delivered design goods created by Barschel's colleague. As Barschel remembered, "Hitler then went into one of his famous tantrums, stomping around the room and eventually dropping to the floor and pretty much chewing on the carpet. I was soon ushered out."[10] This frightening experience deepened Barschel's ongoing disgust of the Nazis and strengthened his attitude toward leaving Germany.

Below, left to right
Cover of Eigen-Marken publication showing
twenty graphic brand marks by members of
the Deutscher Werkbund. Roger Remington
Collection.

"Immer Schneller (Always Faster) Deutsche
Reichsbahn," German National Railway,
no date, poster, 42.7 × 32 cm.

Barschel continued to be enamored by the visual potential of
the railroad, and this became a common subject of interest in
his design and his business. Now practicing design in Berlin,
opening his own studio there in 1935, he was soon working
as head designer for the German Government Railroad.
One project of particular importance was a poster for a
major automobile exhibit in Berlin. In the world of Berlin
graphic designers, Barschel's star was rising. A 1935 issue of
the German design magazine *Gebrauschsgraphik* featured
Barschel's Berlin work.

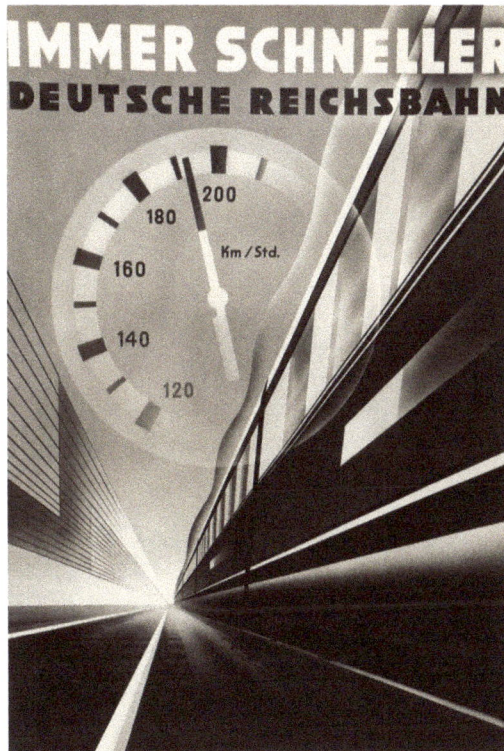

11 Larson, *In the Garden of Beasts*, 56.

Graphic Design: An Emerging Style

Beyond the difficult geopolitical climate of the times, Berlin was *the* cultural place to be in Barschel's formative days because it was geographically the meeting place of the East and West. "Nicely dressed men and women sat in the Romanisches Café drinking coffee and wine, and smoking cigarettes and cigars, and exercising the sharp wit for which Berliners were famous–the Berliner schnauzer."[11] A hotbed of progressive creative energy was present in many art forms, such as music, painting, architecture, design, and film. Berlin was the epicenter of European creativity. El Lisstizky, the Russian artist/designer, spoke German and traveled frequently to Germany, bringing the ideas of Constructivism and avant-garde sensibilities. He inspired Barschel and others–including Jan Tschichold, Kurt Schwitters, and the graphic designers of the Ring Neuer Werbegestalter (Circle of Modern Advertising Designers)– especially in their use of typography.

The Bauhaus was Germany's most recognized design school, but quite separate from this, there existed in Berlin an equally established group of graphic designers, many of whom were part of the Deutscher Werkbund (German Association of Craftsmen), an association of artists, architects, designers, and industrialists. Established in 1907, the Werkbund became an important element in the development of Modernist design in Germany. Among its members were Valentin Zietara, Hans Schleger, Alfred Mahlau, Lucien Bernhard, and William Deffke. These designers, along with Barschel's teachers O.H.W. Hadank, Ernst Boehm, and George Salter, had a profound influence on the young designer.

Deutscher Werkbund mark.
Roger Remington Collection.

"Ein Meisterwerk Deutscher Technik"
(A Masterpiece of German Technology),
German National Railway, no date, poster,
42.7 × 32 cm.

**"Life is like a train ride. The passengers
on the train are seemingly going to the
same destination as you, but based on
their belief in you or their belief that
the train will get them to their desired
destination they will stay on the ride
or they will get off somewhere during
the trip."**

JohnA Passaro

12 Remington, personal video
    interview with Hans Barschel, 1984.

Below, left to right
Cassandre (Adolphe Mouron) (1901–1968)
© ARS, NY, "Etoile du Nord," 1927, poster,
75 × 105 cm. Photo courtesy of the Estate
of A.M. CASSANDRE/Art Resource, NY.

Cassandre (Adolphe Mouron) (1901–1968)
© ARS, NY, "Triplex," 1930, poster, 80 ×
120 cm & 120 × 160 cm. Photo courtesy
of the Estate of A.M. CASSANDRE/Art
Resource, NY.

Evolution: More Formative Influences

Barschel's early design work was also influenced by French
poster designer AM Cassandre, a pseudonym for Adolphe
Jean-Marie Mouron. Barschel took an extended trip through
England, France, and Switzerland to study European poster
art. While visiting Paris on this European jaunt, he discovered
and admired even more of Cassandre's street posters.
He recalled: "On one of the empty walls of the Galleries
Lafayette department store, I saw the first Cassandre, which
I so admired. It was a lady with a summer hat and very
graciously executed, and she was standing there. And I loved
it. It was fantastic. And then I saw his travel poster of the
French north star train called 'Étoile du Nord.'"[12]

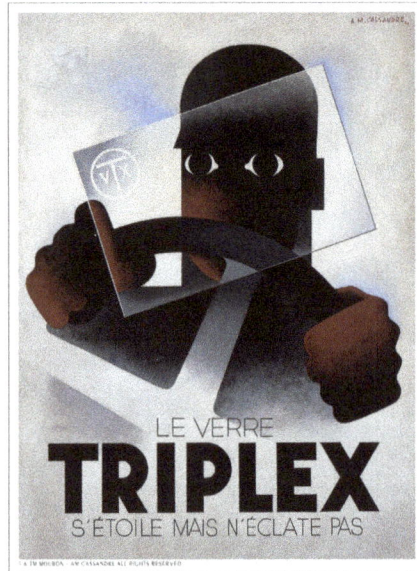

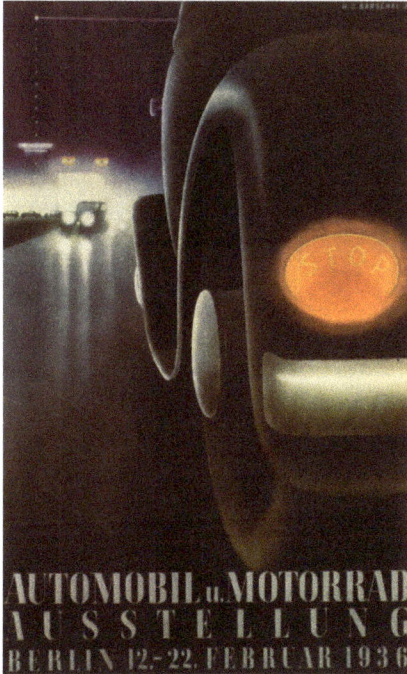

Poster design for an automobile exhibition in Berlin, 1936, 12.6 × 19.5 cm

13 Remington, personal video interview with Hans Barschel, 1984.

Cassandre became his idol, and Barschel was able to meet him. Cassandre soon befriended young Barschel, commenting that, for him, the poster was "art that had gone out on the street."[13] Cassandre gave Barschel one of his famous posters titled "Triplex," which promoted auto safety glass. He personalized the gift by signing the poster "for Ha-Jo Barschel. AM Cassandre."

The posters of other French artists Jean Carlu, Paul Colin, and Charles Loupot also made an impression on the touring Barschel. These graphic forms and shapes, now referred to as the Art Deco style, greatly expanded Barschel's emerging visual aesthetic. As a movement, Art Deco was inspired by Art Nouveau, the Bauhaus, and other formal visual forces such as the kinetic forms of the ballet. Barschel was not the only designer whose work was influenced by this form. His notable contemporaries—such as Alexey Brodovitch, Herbert Bayer, Joseph Binder, Leonetto Cappiello, and, later, E. McKnight Kauffer—also found inspiration in Art Deco. Two other art movements of the time were important in Barschel's work. Purism, influenced by architect Le Corbusier and artist Amadee Ozenfant, represented objects as elementary forms devoid of detail. Surrealism, originating in Italy, was dominated by imagery from dream landscapes and the expression of forms from the unconscious. Barschel's graphics integrated these influences as collage-like compositions of various objects and subject matter, all extending and communicating the intended message.

14 Smithsonian Archives of American Art, Oral History interview with Hans Barschel, 1994.

15 Remington, personal interview with Hans Barschel, 1985.

"New York – Welcome to the land of freedom – An ocean steamer passing the Statue of Liberty," *Frank Leslie's Illustrated Newspaper*, July 2, 1887, wood engraving, Library of Congress Prints and Photographs Division.

Immigration: Coming to America

Barschel was always intellectually curious. He loved to ask questions and challenge established norms. A common theme in his quest for personal meaning was thinking about his destiny in life. Berlin was in crisis, and this gave him cause for great reflection. With the dramatic rise of Hitler and the National Socialist Party (Nazis), the young Barschel became ever more politically disenchanted with his life and future in Germany.

> I had a prediction from a gypsy girl when I was nine years old. I was on vacation on the island of Rügen with my aunt who was my mother's sister. We went on a Sunday walk. Suddenly we saw a camp of gypsies there. A young lady came towards us in some sort of a dancing step and asked my aunt, strangely enough, for permission to read my palm. She predicted my life all the way to America. It was unbelievable. She told me that things in Germany would get very rough and I must get out. I would know when to depart at the time I heard a certain song.[14]

Shortly thereafter, in Berlin, he heard an organ grinder in the distance playing "Sonny Boy" and other American tunes. "I got to him and gave the organ grinder a tip. A Mark bill. I said to him, 'You gave me the audible signal. You don't know it, but I'm going to America.'"[15]

Barschel became increasingly disgusted with Nazism. On a jaunt in a park in Berlin, he was saddened to discover, over the horizon and disguised by trees, rows and rows of tanks that were present and ready for war. The fact that Barschel was about to be inducted into the army also prompted his urgency to leave Germany. Professionally, he saw little chance for progress in Europe. Later he reflected, "I got the hell out of Germany before it blew up." When asked if he was afraid to leave Germany, he said, "I was actually happy because I was on my way to accomplishing what I wanted to do."[16] He felt that in America he would find personal freedom and the external stimulation necessary for doing good work and for continued development.

At his departure from the train station, his family was there to see him off. He was using forged travel documents, and his trip by train out of Germany on April 29, 1937, was not a smooth experience. A Nazi officer happened to be riding in the same compartment and created a very tense situation for those sharing the cramped space. The officer sternly ordered a young man in the car to "get his feet off the seat." The tense train trip to Holland continued, but it was springtime, and seeing the fields of blooming tulips from the train window was a relief. Soon Barschel sailed for London by way of Amsterdam.

16 Remington, personal interview with Hans Barschel, 1985.

Enroute: A London Prediction

Once he arrived in England, Barschel's fast train brought him directly to London. At that time, departing Germans were not allowed to take financial assets out of the country, so Barschel had left Berlin wearing the most expensive clothes he could purchase. (Not thinking ahead, he would eventually arrive in New York on a warm spring day, quite uncomfortable with the heat from his costly, yet heavy, German overcoat.)

While spending a three-day layover in London, waiting for the boat to America, he was hesitant to venture out because of his limited English language skills.

London, Nelson's Column at Trafalgar Square. Coward_lion / Adobe Stock.

"London goes beyond any boundary or convention. It contains every wish or word ever spoken, every action or gesture ever made, every harsh or noble statement ever expressed. It is illimitable. It is Infinite London."

Peter Zackroyd

I looked out of the hotel window, and there was hardly any of the red buses still going there as the rush hour was over. In the distance I could see Trafalgar Square with the famous Nelson obelisk. I was drawn to this and went out of the hotel and down the street and walked to the monument. I looked around and saw older, retired men sitting around the fountain. Suddenly a man spoke to me, speaking cockney. I could hardly understand him yet I somehow managed. It all seemed strange to me.

He was like an average gentleman and he said to me, "You come from the Continent." The English always say that whoever comes from Europe is from "the Continent." And he addressed me as "governor." It was so amusing to me. He said, "You will be on your way to another continent, you will be very successful there, and you will like it. Here in 1939, there will be terrible air raids, bombardments from the sky, and this church, this will go up in flames, but don't you worry; it's all going to be rebuilt." He told me already, then, "that Hitler would lose the war." As I turned to him, he was gone. He just disappeared. Looking back many years later, I remembered this incident as though I had talked to God in Trafalgar Square. It was like that. It was just unbelievable.[17]

18 Remington, personal interview with
Hans Barschel, 1985.

Below

Samuel H. Gottscho, "River House, 52nd
St. and E. River, New York City. Cloud study,
noon, looking south from 27th floor,"
1931, 12.7 × 17.8 cm. Gottscho-Schleisner
Collection, Library of Congress,
Prints and Photographs Division.

**"I like to be in New York. It is still
a wonderful catastrophe, but inspiring."**

Le Corbusier

America: The Creative Forties

New York City, otherwise known as the Big Apple, is famous
for its hustle—"the city that never sleeps"—its tall buildings,
and its cultural importance. It was known for the colorful
Mayor Fiorello LaGuardia, crime and mob activity, and cheap
hotels. In fact, a room at the Hotel Lexington was three
dollars a night.[18] The Empire State and Chrysler buildings
commanded the skyline. As the country emerged slowly from
the Great Depression, among many Americans there was a
sense of optimism and even anticipation.

The World's Fair in Flushing Meadows was being planned to
present a vision of a modern "world of tomorrow," with its
futuristic exhibits, architecture, and events.

Artist unkown, United States postage stamp commemorating the New York World's Fair, 1939.

19 Remington, personal interview with Hans Barschel, 1985.

After his voyage to America via the Cunard Lines, on May 9, 1937, at the age of twenty-five, Hans Barschel arrived with seventy-five cents to his name and knowing very little English. After seeing the Statue of Liberty, he was met at the pier by a cousin.

As was typical for immigrants at that time, before his formal naturalization process was completed and in order to stay in the United States, he had to travel to Cuba and then reenter the United States. In September, he proceeded to Miami but was advised that he would need $500 to get into Cuba. He made a hurried phone call to a friend in New York; this was followed by the money to allow Barschel to proceed. He recalled that he and his colleagues were finally welcomed in New York because "so many good designers were coming to America from Europe."[19] Again, it was a matter of being in the right place at the right time. With the waning of the Great Depression, American business was ready for new ideas, modern directions, and fresh talent ready to meet their marketing-communications goals. Barschel and his immigrant colleagues were ready for the challenge.

Initially living in Forest Hills, it became clear to Barschel that if he were to succeed with living and with practicing design professionally, he had to learn English. He soon found that he could quickly learn English by spending his free time in movie theaters on Times Square, watching the newsreel films over and over again–all day for twenty-five cents. Early on, he was supported by a cousin and his former Berlin teacher George Salter, already established as a book designer in New York.

At right
United Airlines poster design, from *PM* magazine volume 4, number 6, May 1938. 14 × 19.7 cm.

Below, left to right
Cover design for *PM* magazine volume 4, number 6, May 1938, 22 × 14.5 cm.

New York Central poster design, from *PM* magazine volume 4, number 6, May 1938, 14 × 19.7 cm.

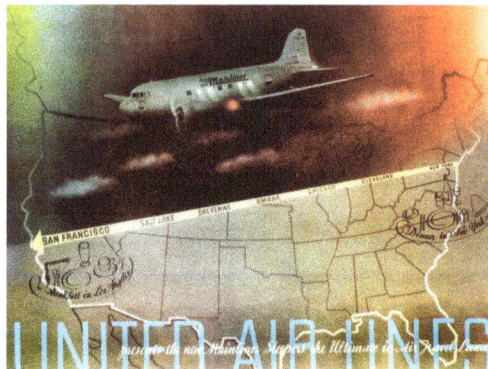

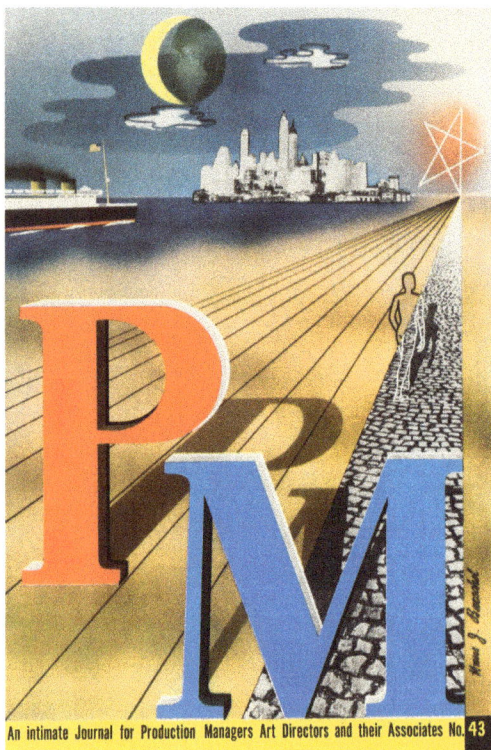

Above, left to right
Hans Barschel atop Rockefeller Center
soon after his arrival from Europe.
Roger Remington Collection.

Self-promotional brochure, no date,
19.5 × 13 cm.

Salter's brother Stephan introduced Barschel to Dr. Robert Leslie. A medical doctor by training, Leslie had a great love for typography, printing, and the graphic arts. Known as "Doctor Bob" to his associates, Leslie owned a major New York typography company, The Composing Room, Inc. This firm supplied quality typesetting for advertising and printing firms. Leslie's shop was the first stop for many aspiring designers, especially those arriving from Europe. He welcomed the many ex-patriate European designers during these years by giving them encouragement, referrals for new clients, exhibits at his A-D Gallery, and publicity through his graphic arts journal, *PM* (later to be called *AD*). Many immigrant designers, such as Will Burtin, Herbert Bayer, Ladislav Sutnar, Dr. M.F. Agha, and others were welcomed and given help by Leslie.

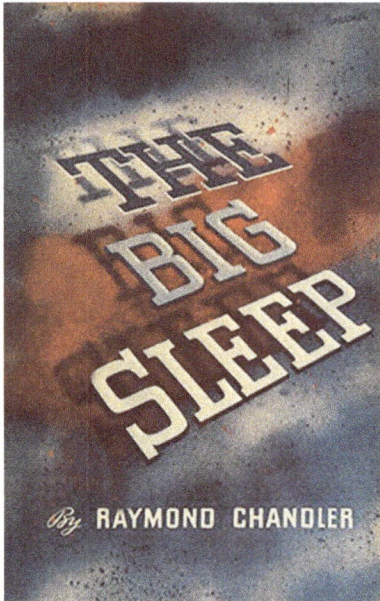

The word on the street was that "there were no good designers in New York except for the immigrants."[20] Paul Rand, Alex Steinweiss, Gene Federico, Lester Beall, and Irvine Kamens were emerging graphic designers who shared a Modernist approach. They also benefited from Leslie's support as they sought to begin their careers. Leslie became a key mentor to an entire generation of rising young Modernist graphic designers.

Eventually, Leslie mounted an exhibit of Barschel's work at the A-D Gallery and devoted an insert highlighting Barschel's work in issue 43 of PM: *An Intimate Journal for Production Managers, Art Directors, and their Associates*. The imagery in this surreal-like cover mirrors Barschel's real-life journey to America. Among the first projects Leslie provided Barschel was an assignment for the Book of the Month Club.

20 Remington, personal interview with Hans Barschel, 1985.

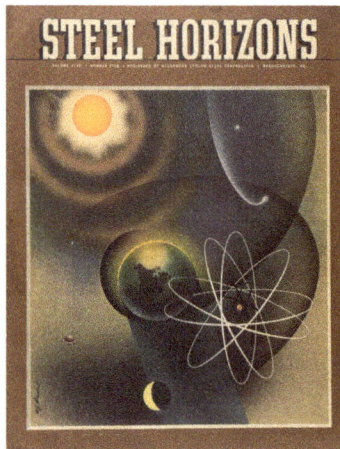

21 Remington, personal video interview with Hans Barschel, 1984.

22 Remington, personal video interview with Hans Barschel, 1984.

Opposite page, top to bottom
Cover design for *The Big Sleep,* Alfred A. Knopf, 1939, 12.7 × 18.7 cm.

Cover design for *Steel Horizons* volume 5, number 5, 1943, 34.5 × 28 cm.

A subscription organization, this business shipped new novels, biographies, and documentaries to serious readers every month. Barschel's experience in book design in Berlin with George Salter gave him a basis for beginning this specialty. Barschel recalled, "Equipped with nothing but my German samples, I was almost everywhere highly complimented about my portfolio."[21] Some art directors found his style too advanced, but his stubborn tenacity eventually led him to a few courageous publishers along Madison Avenue and 57th Street, who felt that "my multidimensional and somewhat Surrealist approach would be just the thing for their mystery-book jackets."[22] He persevered, project by project, until his reputation was established; before long, he was beginning to have a full schedule of assignments, many from prestigious clients.

This page, left to right
Cover design for *Women's Reporter*, 30.5 × 39.5 cm.

Cover design for *More Business*, January 1941, 35.3 × 27.8 cm.

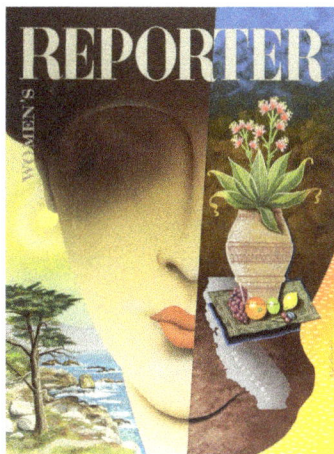

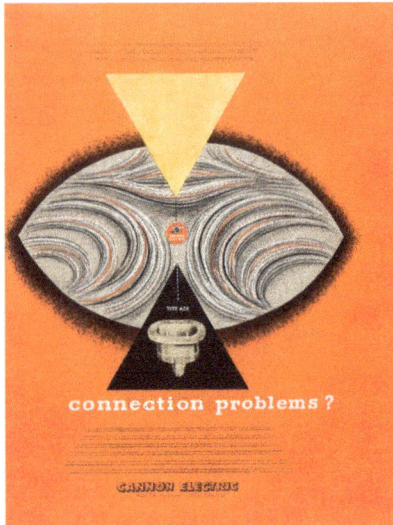

Sketch for a Cannon Electric Co. advertisement, c. 1956, tempera, pencil, paper on red paper mounted on illustration board, 34.3 × 25.4 cm.

Exposure: A Challenge from *Fortune* Magazine

A major professional opportunity soon came to Barschel in the form of designing for a major American magazine. *Fortune*, a global business magazine published by *Time Inc.*, had been founded by Henry Luce in 1930. The cover price then was one dollar, steep when compared to other business magazines that sold for ten cents to twenty-five cents– but they were little more than numbers and statistics printed in black-and-white. *Fortune*, on the other hand, had well-researched articles, photos in color and in black-and-white, original commissioned artwork and design, and abstract Art Deco covers wrapped around an oversized 200-page magazine. Barschel heard that *Fortune* magazine would speculate with new designers and view experimental cover designs. He responded to this opportunity and submitted several proposed designs. One of these covers was accepted, and important professional recognition came to Barschel for his June 1938 *Fortune* magazine cover. For the first time, a view of a modern expressway interchange in Queens was illustrated on the cover of America's major business magazine. Eventually, Barschel was to design four additional covers. Because of his innovative visual-form styling, two covers in 1939 were important in extending *Fortune*'s interest in his work. These cover designs introduced Barschel's use of color, illustration, and composition.

Above, top to bottom
Hans Barschel, 1940s, 25 × 20 cm.

Self-promotion design used to obtain new commercial art clients, from *PM* volume 4, number 6, 1938. Image is used again from the Berlin subway mural project.

In the March issue, he created a cross-section view of the new Wankel engine to accompany an article in the magazine. Also in 1939, a cover showing a dramatic illustration of a storm affecting a windmill detail was accepted. In 1942– during World War II–he designed a cover that showed a view of a prospective target through a submarine periscope. The original art for this cover was later collected by a Navy admiral and went through the Pacific in an aircraft carrier. Finally, in 1948, Barschel created a *Fortune* cover in which he presented multiple views of a postwar car to illustrate an issue on automobile design. These Barschel covers add to the significant lore of *Fortune* magazine covers, which have been such an important documentation of major Modernist designers such as George Giusti, Herbert Bayer, Antonio Petrucelli, Will Burtin, and many more. Just studying the covers of *Fortune* provides, in itself, an American history of graphic design. In 1938, Barschel received an award from AIGA (American Institute of Graphic Arts) for the design of one of his *Fortune* magazine covers.

More and more immigrant designers began working in New York. Barschel recalled that many of his new American clients found him interesting beyond just his talent and innovative design work. They liked the fact that he was personally different–cultured, with a German accent– and had an unusual haircut. His graphic style was a contrast to other American Modernist pioneers like Lester Beall, Bradbury Thompson, and Paul Rand, who concurrently were also starting their careers in New York.

GRAPHIC DESIGN ARCHIVES CHAPBOOK SERIES

23 Remington, personal interview
with Hans Barschel, 1985.

Illustration for poster "For One Peaceful
World," United Nations, water color wash,
airbrush and tempera, 40.6 × 61 cm. Roger
Remington collection. Demonstrates Hans
Barschel's expert use of his ink-wash, hand
graphics, and airbrush technique.

While their work reflected acquired roots in Constructivism, Barschel's Modernist influences were more eclectic, based in Art Deco and Surrealism, as he integrated pictorial and illustrative form in his graphic design solutions. This particular style of integrated imagery was also represented by other European immigrants such as Joseph Binder, Herbert Bayer, George Giusti, and others.

For many, graphic design at this time was an integration of imagery that included representational illustration, hand lettering, symbolic forms, and airbrush transitions. Barschel was a self-taught expert craftsman in combining visual elements and concepts that were imaginative. His technique was flawless. Barschel's design solutions consistently evidenced a strong contrasting feeling of space between foreground and background. The cover design for the *PM* issue exemplifies this spatial effect. His graphic solutions applied rich colors and carefully integrated the pictorial and symbolic elements with the typography. His use of collage and other hand-painted form enhanced his compositions. To be a professional designer, one had to be capable with many techniques. Airbrush was one of Barschel's major skills, having mastered this as a student. He recalled from these student days: "At school in Berlin there was a young man using the airbrush, and I saw it for the first time. I was very impressed with the effects he was creating. He advised me on what kind of airbrush to get and he showed me how to begin. Soon I was in the airbrush business. By the time I was in practice in New York, I was an expert."[23]

Opposite page, left to right, top to bottom
Cover design for *Sharp & Dohme Seminar*,
February 1943, 27.8 × 21.4 cm.

Cover design for *Sharp & Dohme Seminar*,
August 1942, 27.8 × 21.4 cm.

Cover design for *Ciba Symposia*, 1946,
22.8 × 15.6 cm.

Cover design for *Our Scientific World*,
Syracuse, NY: L.W. Singer, 1955–1956,
32.7 × 22.5 cm.

Illustration of a hand, no date, 21 × 16 cm.

24 Remington, personal interview
with Hans Barschel, 1985.

Later, Barschel's sense of humor was evident in this advice
to a student: "There are two things that you never share with
anyone. One is your airbrush, and the other is your wife."[24]
Coupled with the beautiful form transitions afforded by the
airbrush was a mastery of detailed hand painting and lettering.
His design solutions consistently had a sense of realism that
often bordered on qualities of the abstract, yet there was
always a feeling of unity in a Barschel design.

New Technologies: Visualizing the Invisible

The decade of the '40s was a time of opportunity, even with
World War II underway. Then, as America retooled for peace
after 1945, artists, designers, writers, photographers, and
other creative types were in great demand to promote and
advertise the goods and services that were now available.
Barschel was in his element in this dynamic milieu. His
practice was very busy with large-scale assignments, many for
prestigious pharmaceutical clients such as CIBA and Sharp and
Dohme. Advances in technology, particularly in atomic energy,
resulted in a need for designers to visualize invisible processes.
In New York, Barschel, along with another prominent
German immigrant, Will Burtin, pioneered this new imaging
specialty of making comprehensible–through visual form–
processes and aspects of technology. This came to be known
as information design, and Barschel was at the forefront of
pioneering these necessary creative skills.

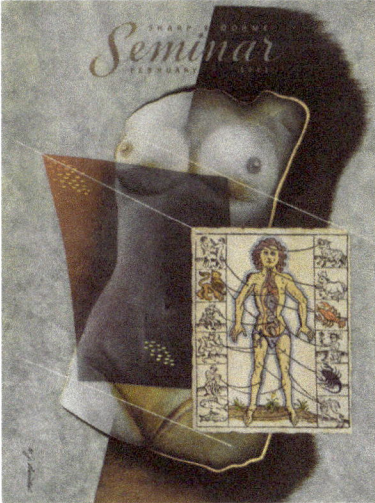

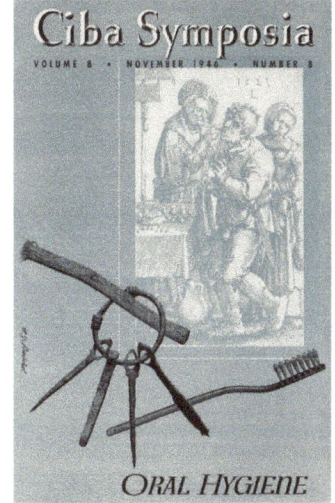

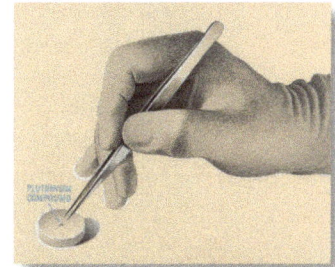

Beyond the Graphics: An Active Social Life

Barschel was part of a German immigrant community in New York. His social friends included many German-speaking expatriates, such as the Dadaist George Grosz, who was known for his satirical and caricature drawings of an earlier Berlin life. Barschel recalled: "At a holiday party on Long Island, I was with Grosz, who was a bit crazy. He had too much to drink and, when leaving the party, walked outside right through the screen door."[25] Dr. Richard Huelsenbeck, a psychiatrist and Dadaist poet, was also part of this circle. Barschel's connections with George and Stephan Salter continued.

Barschel had met a very attractive woman, Marga Erika Werdermann, in 1943. She also was a German immigrant. They met while on summer vacation at Garnet Lake in New York State's Adirondack Mountains. While they were having dinner together at the resort, Marga choked on some very hot food. Barschel came to the rescue by patting her on the back. This was just the beginning. They were married in 1948 and enjoyed forty-six happy years together. Many years later, Barschel recalled: "Marga was a real lady, probably much too good for me. I was so involved with my art. She was the one who married me."[26]

Marga Barschel, wife of Hans Barschel, no date, 12.5 × 10 cm.

25 Smithsonian Archives of American Art,
Oral History interview with
Hans Barschel, 1994.

26 Remington, personal video interview
with Hans Barschel, 1984.

27 Remington, personal video interview
with Hans Barschel, 1984.

Above
Rochester, N.Y. western skyline around
1950. City of Rochester / Rochester Images
digital collection.

"Rochester? Why Rochester?""Why not?"
George Bailey and Sam Wainwright in
conversation, *It's a Wonderful Life*

A New Chapter: The Rochester Years
In the 1940s, the graphic design community in New York
was not large. Barschel's creative work was well known in
the printing, publishing, and advertising worlds, and in 1950
he had a one-man exhibit of his graphic design at the New
York Art Directors Club. His graphics for CIBA Symposia
additionally brought him recognition. A representative from a
large Rochester, New York, printing firm saw Barschel's work
in a magazine and contacted him. This prompted Barschel,
in 1949, after having served two years as the art director at
the New York City Department of Public Health, to consider
a new professional direction. Barschel and his wife, Marga,
decided, "We had had enough of the canyons of New York."[27]
He and Marga moved upstate to begin a new and significant
final chapter in their lives.

Rochester companies such as Eastman Kodak Company, Haloid-Xerox, Pfaudler Permutit, Gleason Works, and Bausch & Lomb were international leaders in their specialties. The city was a thriving business and industrial center with a strong specialization in imaging, photography, and high-quality printing, especially of corporate annual reports. Because of Rochester's reputation in the graphic arts, designers were aware of professional opportunities upstate. In his transition away from New York City, Barschel saw a future for himself as a designer for companies such as Great Lakes Press Corporation and, eventually, John P. Smith Printing Company. By 1954, his progressive ideas about design and his outstanding graphic accomplishments were recognized by printers and others in Rochester.

A Fresh Opportunity: Design at RIT
Rochester Institute of Technology at that time was still very much in the beaux-arts tradition of art education. However, Stanley Witmeyer, the director of RIT's School of Art and Design and a visionary educator, sought to advance RIT to the forefront in design education. A Rochester designer with RIT ties, Bruce Unwin, was acquainted with Barschel through collaboration at a Rochester printing company. He recommended him to Witmeyer, who jumped on the opportunity of adding a new teacher to the faculty, especially as many of the old-guard teachers were retiring. To facilitate this vision, Witmeyer asked Barschel to teach an evening class in advertising design at RIT. The class was very successful, and Witmeyer saw that Barschel could be the nucleus of change and much more than a part-time teacher. Soon thereafter, Barschel was offered a professorship at RIT.

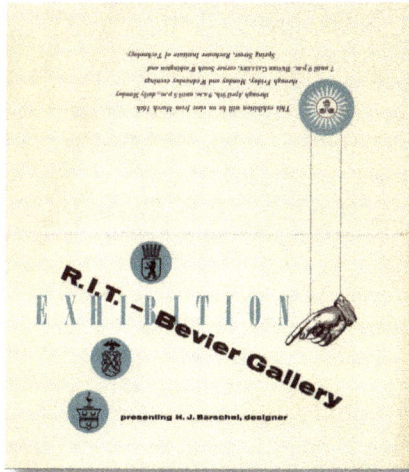

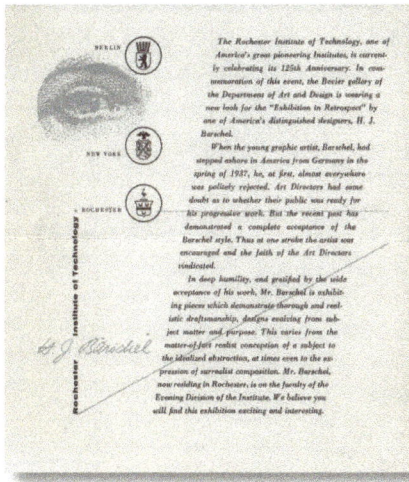

In his new role as a teacher and nurturer of young designers, Barschel flourished. He soon became a major force in the transformation of the design program at RIT. His one-man exhibit in 1954 at RIT's Bevier Gallery documented his fifteen years of graphic design practice and was an important stimulus for colleagues and, particularly, for students. The exhibit showed RIT and the Rochester community the new look and potential of a Modernist program. RIT was now poised to become more than an evening trade school for Rochester industries. It was clear to Barschel that "the most important years of my life were yet to come."[28]

Witmeyer told Barschel, "Forget about anything which we have done in the past. Do it a new way." Barschel curated exhibits of top international designers who were his acquaintances. Exciting posters and printed graphics by AM Cassandre, Will Burtin, E. McKnight Kauffer, Herbert Bayer, Paul Rand, and George Giusti graced the walls of RIT's Bevier Gallery. This exposure at RIT and in Rochester brought the best and the finest of contemporary graphic design work, which served as models for the new direction of the school. In the classroom, Barschel counseled students to adopt, through their assignments, a wider, more humanistic global vision. "We rearranged two classrooms to be set up as a workshop setting so I could handle this like an actual advertising agency studio."[29] Barschel established practical, real-world assignments for his students and moved them into the community to face real problems that dealt with environmental issues and community needs. In Eastman Kodak Company's backyard, he was among the first designer-educators to see the potential of multimedia imaging techniques in presentation and communications.

28 Remington, personal video interview with Hans Barschel, 1984.

29 Remington, personal video interview with Hans Barschel, 1984.

Below
A student field trip to the Finger Lakes for photographic research. Photo by R. Roger Remington. Hans Barschel's class assignments often involved nature field trips to parks and nearby natural resources.

Opposite page
Graphic Design Job Ticket, 1967, 27.5 × 21.5 cm. Barschel organized his teaching to simulate a professional design office.

This work anticipated by many years the use of slideshows as tools in corporate communications.

Although he did not stress technique, he integrated the use of photography as a major element in the graphic designer's tool kit. In his classes, he encouraged students to use photography and to carry a camera at all times. Many students were introduced to new processes and camera formats, such as the then-popular half-frame camera, the Olympus Pen. Having an expensive Exacta 35mm SLR camera around his neck inspired his students to see how a professional was equipped. His interactions with students in class and beyond gave them a context and afforded critical global views of design and the design process. His by-then excellent command of the English language was an important asset in communicating to students and colleagues. He challenged his students to document the construction of Rochester's Midtown Plaza–America's first indoor shopping mall–which was designed by architect Victor Gruen. Many of his class projects for students were based on field trips into natural surroundings.

Graphic Design JOB TICKET

Title Cover design for H O L I D A Y <u>magazine</u>	**Production number** T W O B
Date submitted October 25th, 1967	## Roughs
To Graphic Designers, Senior WORKSHOP	
Client Curtis Publishing Co. Philadelphia, Pa	**Quantity** Several pastel-tissues
J.M.Clifford, Pres., Stephen Kelly, Publ.	**Size** in the original size of mag.cover
Subject Creation of a "forward-looking" de-	**Mat size**
signed or illustrated cover !	**Due date** WED.NOV.1st, 67. 9 AM first crit.
Reproduction method Full color, half-tone letter-	**Media** no limitation!
press... or an advanced offset reproduct-	
ion technique.	## Comps

Information and procedure The cover should depict either New York City as one of the greatest international vacation centers or the follow-ing other vacation spots in our New York S T A T E : The Hudson Valley up to Albany, the Cats Kills along Route 17, the Adiron-dacks, the Thousand Island area, the Ocean Beaches incl.Long Island (Jones Beach etc.) Lake Ontario, the Finger Lakes, the Vine-Yards above Canandaigue Lake, the Cherry-Valley area... or whatever part of New York State you may find worthwhile to spend a Summer <u>or Winter</u> Vacation. SELECT ONLY ONE!	**Quantity**
	Size
	Mat size
	Due date
	Media

DUE NOV. 8th, 3 PM!

Finished Art

Research ... your personal experiences with one of the most colorful States. You could 'feature', for instance, a visu-al reflection of WATKINS GLEN, its canyon-beauty,- its automobile races, et cetera. Remember, New York City is more then just <u>Manhattan and sky-scrapers</u> or <u>Greenwich</u>	**Quantity** one finished comp with logo (Holiday) *Which* **Size** title and subtitle *can be* included. *CHANGED!* **Mat size** YOU agree on ONE mat size and color **Due date** variety for display.
Conference date Village... it's a lot of old, intimate spots with fine restaurants, etc	**Media** Unlimited, incl. painting, print-making, silk-screen, etching. The message determines the technique!
Art director *H. J. Barschel*	

→ **Assignment** <u>o n e</u> "b", because of its unique and unusual character, was not posted. It was given on WED.OCT. 4th, and the 3-dimensional visuals of STAIRCASE DECORATIONS for the ROCHESTER RECREATION BUREAU are due TODAY, WED. OCT.25th at 3 PM to be present-ed to the Bureau before 4 PM. One or two designers of each group will carry their model over to the Civic Center... with OUR compliments !

Title like "A SOPHISTICATED SATINGER'S BEAT" — MIDTOWN MANHATTAN — SUbtitle like "A SOPHISTICATED SATINGER'S BEAT" — Title like LAKE CANANDAIGUA

Below

Exhibition announcement design for "RIT Department of Art and Design Presents E. McKnight Kauffer," 1955, 21 × 16.5 cm. Note Barschel's inclusion of symbols for RIT, and the London Underground. E. McKnight Kauffer was an American designer who chose to live and work in England for most of his career. His posters promoting tourism in Great Britain dominate his oeuvre.

Opposite page

Exhibition announcement design for "Exhibition by 3 of America's Most Outstanding Designers... Will Burtin, George Giusti, Paul Rand," 1950s, 15.9 × 18.4 cm. This exhibition was Hans Barschel introducing Modernist designers to RIT.

Beginning in 1954, exhibitions of work by Barschel's national and international graphic design contemporaries appeared in RIT's Bevier Gallery. Shown in Rochester for the first time, the RIT community was exposed to leading modernist designers such as Will Burtin, George Giusti, Paul Rand, and E. McKnight Kauffer. Later Barschel was even able to have an exhibit of posters by the great French poster designer AM Cassandre.

These exhibits were part of Barschel's personal mission to expose RIT to the best of contemporary graphic design as a way of working to modernize design education at RIT.

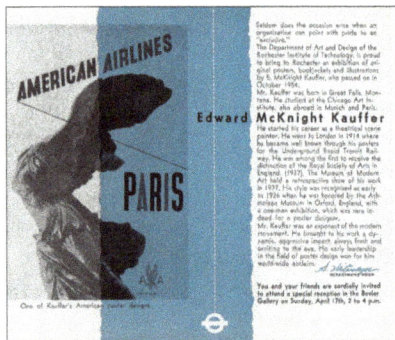

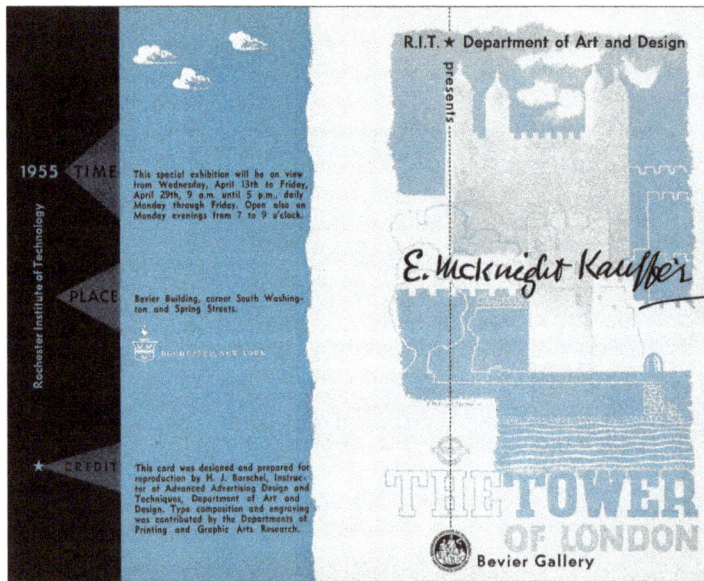

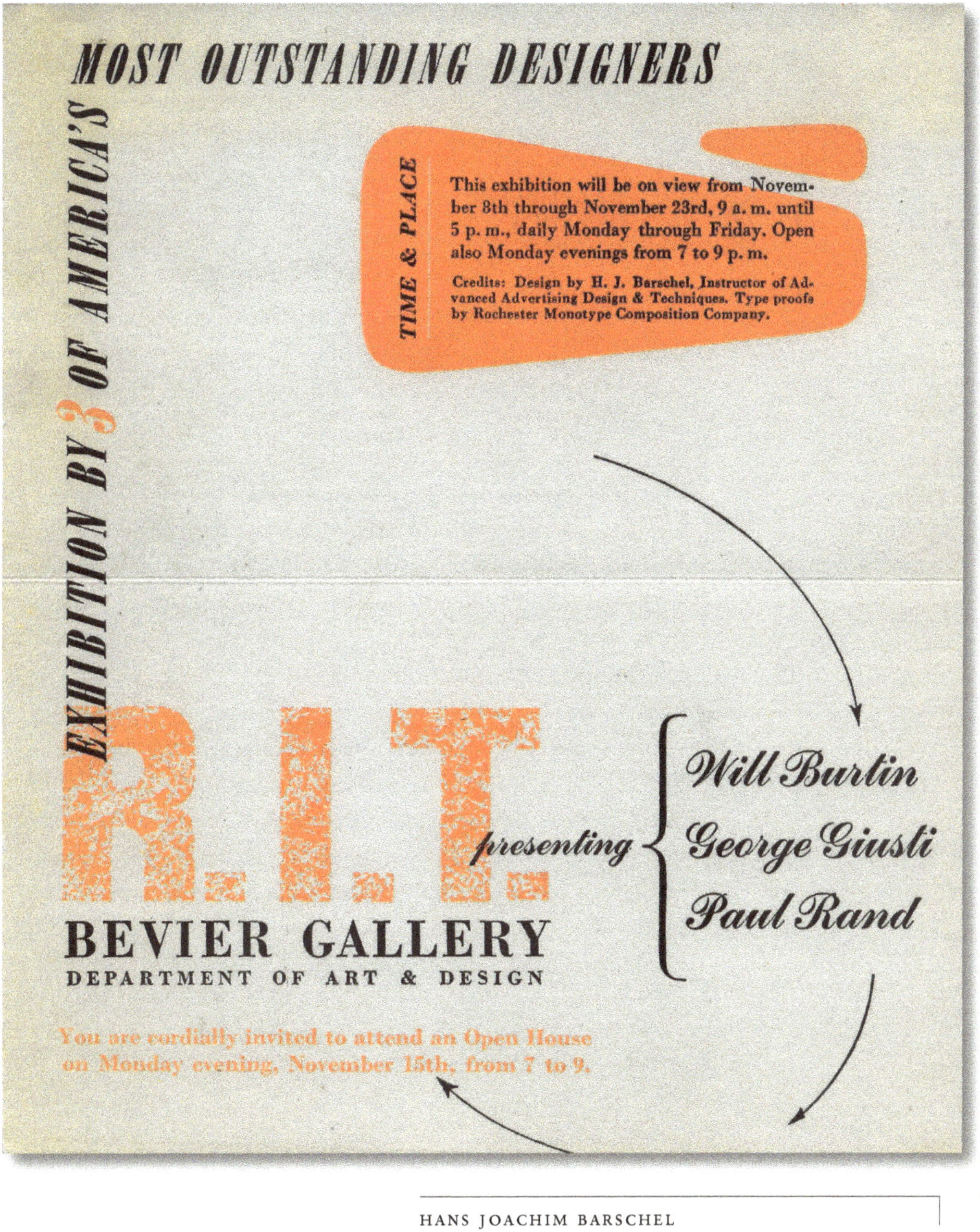

MOST OUTSTANDING DESIGNERS

EXHIBITION BY 3 OF AMERICA'S

TIME & PLACE

This exhibition will be on view from November 8th through November 23rd, 9 a. m. until 5 p. m., daily Monday through Friday. Open also Monday evenings from 7 to 9 p. m.

Credits: Design by H. J. Barschel, Instructor of Advanced Advertising Design & Techniques. Type proofs by Rochester Monotype Composition Company.

R.I.T.

presenting

{ *Will Burtin*
George Giusti
Paul Rand }

BEVIER GALLERY
DEPARTMENT OF ART & DESIGN

You are cordially invited to attend an Open House on Monday evening, November 15th, from 7 to 9.

Communication design "Collage of My Life: Personal Symbols of Evolution," 1975, 7.5 × 11 cm. Collage art for the 713 exhibition.

30 Remington, personal interview with Hans Barschel, 1985.

31 Barschel, "A Plea for Substantialism," *Matrix* 1, no. 1 (1961): 2.

Gene DePrez, a student at the time, recalled, "Hans is fondly remembered by generations of his former students for his generosity, achievements, sense of humor, interests in interdisciplinary studies, global perspective, progressive thinking, generosity of time and attention to their development, and his over-arching optimism." As a teacher, Barschel said, "One must be positive. It is difficult in a chaotic time such as this to be positive. To find your own platform, to understand yourself is the challenge of our time. These students who work here will go on to lead very meaningful lives. The important thing is to be as professional as you can be. This was always my goal."[30]

RIT Opportunities: Creative Collaborations
Barschel was always on the search for opportunities to stretch his own intellectual curiosity. For example, he collaborated with an enlightened colleague, Dr. Maurice Kessman, to produce an innovative tabloid publication called MATRIX, which provided opportunities for more scholarly and experimental ventures into writing, designing, and imaging. Also included in the collaboration were professors R. Roger Remington (author of this book) and Dr. Leonard Barkin. MATRIX was printed at RIT's Graphic Arts Research Center and was an insert in the school newspaper. Kessman wrote in the first issue, "MATRIX seeks people with imagination and vision, who, after having given life to their art, are looking for a way back from their art into life."[31]

Right

Yosaif Cohain, "Prof. Hans J. Barschel, Art School, R.I.T. is seen here photographing Victorian ornamentations during the survey of Palmyra N.Y. last October," c. 1978, photograph, 18 × 18 cm. Photography was a key component in Hans Barschel's work.

Below

StoriGraf diagram, 1969, 21.6 × 27.9 cm. A systematic means for planning visual variables necessary for audio-visual slide presentations. This process later became a corporate communications standard.

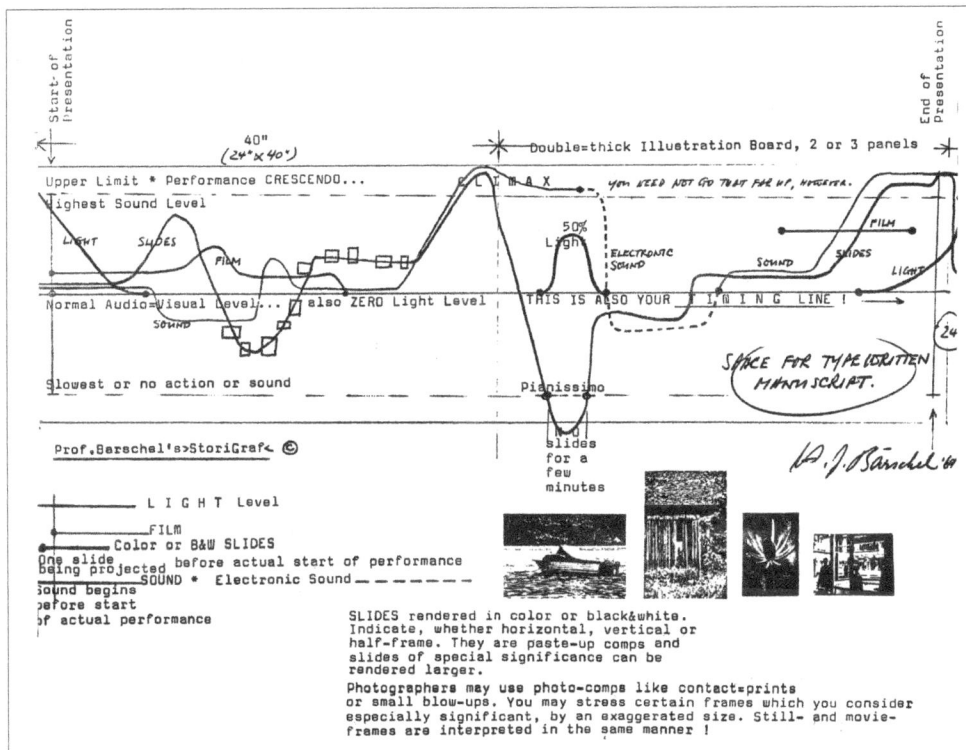

Cover and page from a fundraising brochure for RIT's Graphic Arts Research Department, c. 1954, 22.9 × 15.2 cm.

32 Barschel, "A Plea for Substantialism," 2.

33 Remington, personal video interview with Hans Barschel, 1984.

Later, in a 1961 issue, Barschel contributed a personal article titled "A Plea for Substantialism" in which he concluded, "The mature citizen, by leading a purposeful and substantial life, will be exemplary to the youth of each generation and thus help them to regain strength and faith in the future and to acquire an inner conviction of their mission."[32]

Barschel's design talents brought a whole new brand to RIT's Graphic Arts Research Department. He designed a fundraising brochure in which he included select pieces from his New York City years. These pieces added a sophistication to the publication that was unusual for RIT graphics of the time. His progressive thinking was evident in his personal art and design of the period, as shown publicly at his "713" exhibit in 1965. This exhibit of his personal imagery exposed the community to his new graphic design experiments. The graphic pieces were composed of collage, photographs, and supportive form. The numbers 713 served as a code-number pseudonym for the identification of his exploratory, creative image efforts. Major articles about his work appeared in many magazines, such the feature in the British magazine *Art & Industry* in November 1954, titled "Hans J. Barschel–American Graphic Designer." The article appeared concurrently with Barschel's RIT Bevier Gallery show, "Exhibition in Retrospect," commemorating RIT's 125th anniversary. The exhibit was composed of many selected pieces from Barschel's graphic accomplishments in New York. Above all, through the exhibit, Barschel brought new energy, power, and leadership to the movement toward a distinctive, progressive design education at RIT. He always said, "It has always been my goal to look forward and upward."[33]

Brochure for Barschel's RIT exhibition "713: Hans Barschel exposes his graphic design experimentations," 1965.

Hans Barschel at the opening of the 713 exhibition, 1965.

34 Remington, personal video interview with Hans Barschel, 1984.

Growth: A Connection with the Natural World

Hans Barschel's great love of nature was central to his life as it was to his nurturing qualities as a teacher. He loved to take his classes on trips to find inspiration for creating drawings, photographs, and designs to bring back to the classroom. He was a nurturer in other important ways. A consummate gardener, he loved to say that he was happiest when "he had his hands in the soil."[34] His small personal home garden, so impeccably maintained, became a personal masterpiece of design. His generosity and dedication was apparent when RIT was building its new campus in Henrietta. He obtained permission to move plants and shrubs from his home garden to the tentative nursery on the new campus property.

Hans Barschel in Mendon Ponds Park. Photo by R. Roger Remington.

Hans Barschel planting at the RIT new campus garden nursery, 1960s, 12 × 8.2 cm.

35 Remington, personal video interview with Hans Barschel, 1984.

36 Remington, personal interview with Hans Barschel, 1985.

This love of gardening was to find a connection to his RIT students in the Tojo Memorial Garden project. Barschel and his wife, Marga, were very fond of Yasuji Tojo, an international student in photography who was in his design class. They had him over for dinner often, attempting to understand Japanese culture and celebrating special occasions together. Sadly, in 1974 Tojo was killed in an automobile accident. On campus, a desire arose to honor this young man. In Japan, his family also wished to memorialize their son. They were owners of a large photo-finishing business in Tokyo. Barschel was instrumental in bringing together the idea of a Tojo memorial garden, featuring a stone lantern, sent from Japan and donated by his parents, as its centerpiece. To realize the project, Barschel led committees, gathered support from faculty and staff, wrote proposals, and contributed many special plants and trees from his own garden to the cause. In fact, a mature birch tree, which now towers over the garden, was moved from the Barschel backyard garden at the suggestion of Marga Barschel. On its completion, Barschel wrote, "The garden symbolizes the idea of moving forward, how barren land blooms with nature, given time. It preserves the identity of students who did not have the opportunity to experience the fulfillment of their lives due to war or other tragedies."[35] The beautiful Yasuji Tojo Memorial Garden, adjacent to the Gannett Building, has for years been one of the environmental highlights of the RIT campus. The garden is a green oasis and "softens" the campus's geometric brutalist architecture. Satisfied with his contribution, Barschel called this international garden "the green heart of the sober Brick City."[36]

GRAPHIC DESIGN ARCHIVES CHAPBOOK SERIES

In April of 1975, he published "The Yasuji Tojo Story" to ensure that this history wasn't forgotten. Later he published a second article titled "A Living Memorial of Eternal Youth."

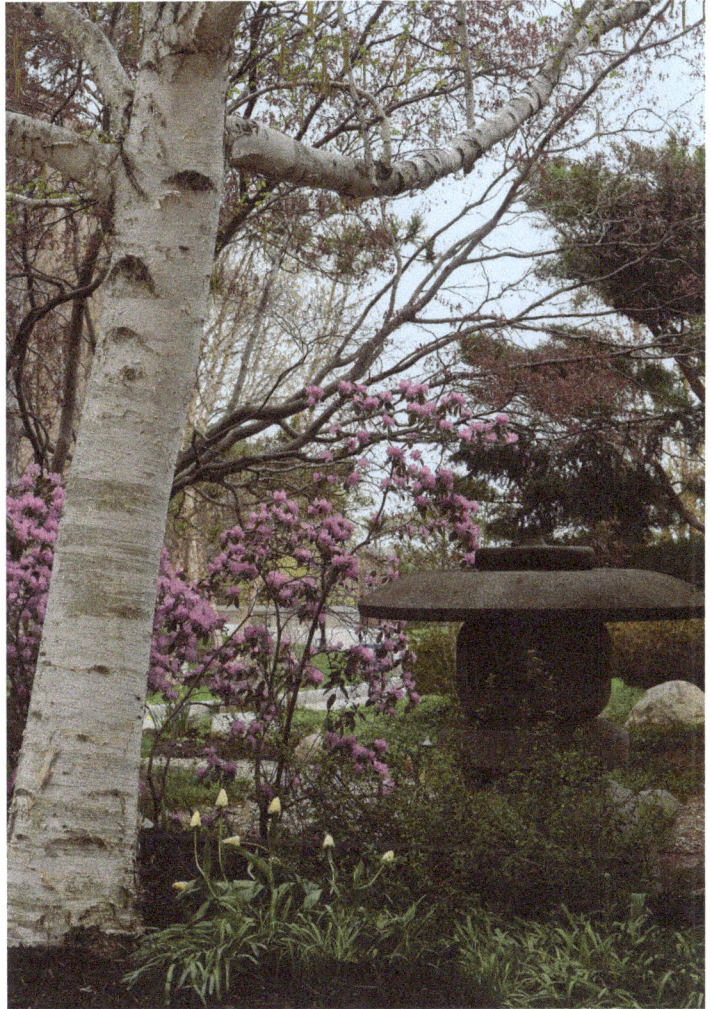

The memorial Japanese lantern at RIT's Tojo garden. RIT Photo Services. For students and faculty, the Tojo Garden is an oasis on the RIT campus.

Hans Barschel often used his own work and that of others to demonstrate a point to an inquiring student. Roger Remington Collection.

Unending Experimentation: A Spiritual Life

Throughout his life, Hans Barschel was spiritual and philosophical, but not in a traditional way.

When Hans Barschel was young, his father used to take him for walks through the parks of Berlin and remind him: "Never sin against nature, because nature is God."[37]

His Aunt Else in Berlin was also a very supportive emotional figure in his developing years. In 1974, reflecting back on his long life, he referred to God often in remembering his experiences. When Barschel was in his eighties, the Rochester *Democrat and Chronicle* newspaper explored this belief in an article titled, "Nature Is a Religion for Brighton Artist."[38]

As one might suspect from the designer Barschel, his search for the creative process was expressed both in verbal and visual form. He wrote, "In my explorations I have found so many specific instances in the arts which are evidence that man must be constantly receiving such subliminal commands or radiation stimuli."[39]

He called this process of creative sources his personal "probing into the unknown" or "Exploits into the Neo-Cosmos." As he probed deeper into the realm of organic, nonobjective form, he discovered its basis in natural processes. The abstract artwork he made during this period of self-searching mirrors powerful compositions of shape and color afforded by media such as painting, photography, and collage. He summed it up, "Yet, no mortal will ever surpass the conceptual daring, the colors and shapes – the creative imagination of the Infinite Mind (God)!"[40]

37 Remington, personal interview with Hans Barschel, 1985.

38 Bullard, "Nature Is Religion for Brighton Artist," *Democrat and Chronicle*, March 6, 1991, E-1.

39 Smithsonian Archives of American Art, Oral History interview with Hans Barschel, 1994.

40 Remington, personal video interview with Hans Barschel, 1984.

GRAPHIC DESIGN ARCHIVES CHAPBOOK SERIES

Caring And Completion: The Final Years

Professionally, Barschel continued to stay active.
A 1952 issue of *Gebrauschsgraphik*, from Germany, featured a major article about Barschel's work. Then, a 1968 issue of the prestigious Japanese design journal IDEA, the premier magazine of international advertising art, included his work in a comprehensive presentation of his contemporaries. The issue included a major showing in color of select Barschel graphics. He was in good company: Included in this historic issue were many of his American contemporaries, such as Paul Rand, Lester Beall, and Alex Steinweiss, as well as fellow immigrant designers, such as Will Burtin, George Giusti, and Herbert Bayer. The issue commemorated the exhibit "A Generation of Graphic Art," which was held at Dr. Leslie's Gallery 303 in New York. The exhibit featured a thirty-year retrospective history of modern graphic design and caused quite a sensation in that world. It introduced systematically the evolution of American graphic design in relation to business and industry in the United States. For Barschel, it was a significant recognition of his fifteen years of professional design accomplishments in New York.

Barschel both designed for freelance clients and brought his talents to bear on upgrading many RIT publications. In 1975, his work was also shown in NOVUM magazine, an offshoot of *Gebrauschsgraphik*. Rochester's AIGA chapter featured, in 1983, a profile article on Barschel, which was part of a series, "Celebrating our Design Heroes," written by one of Barschel's former students, then-RIT Professor R. Roger Remington.

41 Remington, personal video
   interview with Hans Barschel, 1984.

In 1985, he received an award from the Centro Studi E Delle Nazioni in Italy, and in 1990, Barschel was nominated "Man of the Year" by the American Biographical Institute, receiving a certificate and gold medal. This was followed in 1991 by receipt of a gold medal from the International Biographical Association in Cambridge, England.

Prien, K., Sketch of Hans Barschel, 1932, 20 × 17 cm.

Hans Barschel retired from RIT as Professor Emeritus in 1976. His early mentor and devoted friend, Dr. Bob Leslie, then in his late nineties, sent a note saying, "You deserve the honor of a great and devoted teacher. My best wishes on your retirement from active classroom work."[41] Barschel's final years were occupied with his home garden, photographing nature, and travel. He loved to accompany colleagues on trips to Toronto, where he relished the more cosmopolitan atmosphere, recalling often his European beginnings.

Barschel's beloved wife, Marga, passed away in 1989. After his passing in 1998, two close friends, following Barschel's wishes, traveled to his beloved Adirondacks for a memorial remembrance in the same place where he originally vacationed with Marga in 1943.

After his retirement, Hans Barschel occasionally visited the RIT campus. He is shown here with Professors Stanley Witmeyer (left) and R. Roger Remington (right). Roger Remington Collection.

His High Calling Preserved: A Barschel Collection

Since 1983, RIT has made a priority of collecting and preserving the archives of pioneering designers, especially those who shaped the emergence of Modernism in America. Throughout his career, Barschel was always a freelance designer. This meant that all of his original designs were returned to him after production and remained his property. Therefore, he preserved the complete archive of his original work.

Between 1991 and 1994, Barschel worked with RIT Art & Photography Librarian Barbara Polowy to prepare his career archive for donation to the Cary Graphic Design Archive at RIT. Additional work was donated in 1998 and in 2023. The Barschel collection provides a rare look into pre-World War II graphic design in Germany, the emergence of Modernist graphic design in America in the 1940s, and the evolution of RIT's School of Art and Design into a Modernist educational program. It preserves Barschel's place of honor among the forty-five other collections of his contemporaries in the Cary Graphic Design Archive.

AFTER REPRODUCTION, PLEASE, RETURN ORIGINAL TO: H.J. BARSCHEL, 415 East 58ᵗʰ Street, NEW YORK 22, N.Y.

A note that Hans Barschel included on all his original designs to ensure they would be returned to him after production and remain his property.

Portrait of Hans Barschel, c. 1970s.
3.5 × 2.5 cm.

A Lasting Impact: Framing the Barschel Accomplishments

Hans Barschel's legacy is intertwined with his innovative personal contributions to the graphic design world and with the history and evolution of Modernist design education at RIT. A great technological university depends on its faculty to bring meaningful content to its students. Hans Barschel was at the leading edge of both education and design practice. As an immigrant to America, he brought innovative ideas and form to the American design scene. This was realized in the New York City years through his promotional and collateral work. Now is the time to celebrate his accomplishments and frame his story as a significant Modernist design pioneer of his generation.

Looking Back: A Personal Note

It has been an honor to produce this publication honoring Professor Hans Barschel. When I arrived at RIT in 1954, my life experience was limited. I had grown up in a middle-class home in a small city in Upstate New York. I knew I was interested in art, but had no way of finding out what to do with this, or where to go with it. A former classmate directed me to RIT, and, suddenly, I had a direction with promise. Upon my arrival at RIT, Hans Barschel was one of my teachers. This was the next major step in my development as a designer and the beginning of a lifelong relationship.

Hans Joachim Barschel with RIT Professor R. Roger Remington, his friend, colleague, and protégé. The two serigraphs on the wall were created by R. Roger Remington and given to Barschel as a gift. Roger Remington Collection.

With his German charm, knowledgeable manner, and warm humor, he proceeded to open my naïve eyes to the world. Barschel gave me, an innocent kid from a small town, a global view of life—and of design. He established in me a thorough sense of professionalism, tenacity, and what it meant to be a designer. It was the ideal time for me to be at RIT because the school was dramatically changing into a modern design program under Director Stanley Witmeyer. Barschel had recently joined the faculty, and soon he became a major force in this change. In a way, I had the best of both worlds: exposure to the best of the traditional art school faculty and, at the same time, being stretched to Modernist views with the newcomers like Barschel. I was Barschel's student first and then, a few years later, on my return to RIT, he was my colleague, mentor, and friend, since by then we were both on the faculty. This connection endured for many years we worked together and became even closer. It felt as though Hans was a surrogate father to me, and I was a son to him. Other colleagues resented our close working relationship.

Years later, when Barschel was retired and, as my career had unfolded, I was fortunate to travel to Berlin; it was my great pleasure, on my return, to share with my mentor my adventures in Germany. He so enjoyed the connection and learning that, while in Berlin, I had even found his family home in Charlottenberg. I remain thankful to Hans Barschel for opening my eyes to so much in life and for simply being my friend.

R. Roger Remington

BIBLIOGRAPHY

Barschel, Hans J. "A Plea for Substantialism." *Matrix*. 1, no. 1 (Winter 1961): 2–3.

Bullard, Janice. "Nature Is Religion for Brighton Artist." Rochester *Democrat and Chronicle*, March 6, 1991, sec. E: 1–2.

Friedrich, Otto. *Before the Deluge–A Portrait of the 1920s*. New York: Harper Perennial, 1972.

"Hans J. Barschel–American Graphic Designer." *Art & Industry* (November 1954): 160–165.

Heller, Steven. "O.H.W. Hadank, The Classicist Even a Modernist Could Love." Unpublished essay. Message to the author. December 2, 2021.

Kessman, Maurice. *Matrix* 1, no. 1 (Winter 1961).

Larson, Erik. *In the Garden of Beasts: Love, Terror, and an American Family in Hitler's Berlin*. New York: Crown Publishers, 2011.

Mendelsohn, Erich. *Amerika: Bilderbuch eines Architekten.* Berlin: Rudolf Mosse, ed. 1928.

Oral History Interview with Hans Barschel, 1994 September 14. Archives of American Art, Smithsonian Institution. Accessed February 12, 2022.

Remington, R. Roger. *Personal Interview* 1. 1984.

Remington, R. Roger. *Personal Interview* 2. 1985.

Schwaar, Lauren. "Difficulties Faced by Immigrants and Refugees." *Life and Light Magazine.* 2015. Accessed January 17, 2022.

Sharp, Alison, and Elana Shapira. *Émigré Cultures and New Design Dimensions.* New York: Bloomsbury, 2017.

ACKNOWLEDGMENTS

Dr. Bruce Austin
Jim Banlay
Gene DePrez
Dr. Steven Galbraith
Steven Heller
Alexandra Hoff
Amelia Hugill-Fontanel
Dorie Jennings
Dr. Kelly Norris Martin
Bruce Ian Meader
Jan Naujokas
Leigh Remington
M. Suzanne Remington
Marnie Soom
Elizabeth Torgerson-Lamark
A. Sue Weisler

ABOUT THE AUTHOR

R. Roger Remington

R. Roger Remington is the Vignelli Distinguished Professor of Design Emeritus and the former director of the Vignelli Center for Design Studies at Rochester Institute of Technology (RIT) in Rochester, New York. He was on the faculty at RIT for fifty-seven years. As a teacher/scholar, his critical interests are in graphic design history, research, and writing. His deep commitment to design history and preservation has led him to bring the archives of designers of the American Modernist generation to RIT. More recently, in 2010, he was instrumental in the establishment of the Vignelli Center for Design Studies, which houses the career archive of designers Massimo and Lella Vignelli and other designers. He has written five books on designers and design history, with a new book titled *Communicating Knowledge Visually: Will Burtin's Scientific Approach to Information Design* published by RIT Press in 2021.

COLOPHON

Editorial	Alexandra Hoff
Design	Bruce Ian Meader
Production	Marnie Soom
Typefaces	Sabon designed by Jan Tschichold and Frutiger designed by Adrian Frutiger
Series Editor	Dr. Kelly Norris Martin

www.ingramcontent.com/pod-product-compliance
Lightning Source LLC
Chambersburg PA
CBHW061226270326
41928CB00024B/3346